Your life as a Christian is like a journey, a daily walk that you take with God. You got a good start on that journey when you received Jesus Christ as your personal savior, but there is something more that God wants to do in you. There is an important next step in your Christian walk.

As you continue to travel with Christ, you'll discover many new things about yourself, and you will arrive at the point of becoming a completely new person, just as God wants you to be. In order to get there, something will be required of you. You will need to keep going, continually keeping in step with God.

You're off to a good start. Now let's see about your next step.

Your New Direction

When you decided to follow Christ, you made a decision about the direction of your life. You stepped out of a crowd that was moving in the wrong direction and decided to go a different way. Jesus put it this way: "Wide is the gate and broad is the road that leads to destruction, and many enter through it. But small is the gate and narrow the road that leads to life, and only a few find it" (Matthew 7:13–14). You are now walking on the road that leads to life.

Eternal life in heaven is your final destination. But before you get there, God intends for you to live a full, rich, and effective life here on earth. Jesus tells us that the reason He came to earth is that we might have life, and have it to the full (John 10:10). Your next step with Christ will be a major milestone in developing your spiritual life. It will lead you into that full life, and that is something you can experience right now.

How has the direction of your life changed since you accepted Christ?

What clues do you see that people who do not know Christ are headed in a different direction than you are?

Are you longing for something more in your journey with Christ?

What Happened When You Became A Christian

Do you remember when you accepted Jesus Christ into your life? No doubt you experienced a sense of freedom, peace, and joy. What really happened that day?

When you confessed your sins and placed your faith in Jesus Christ, God immediately began to apply the benefits of Christ's sacrifice to you.

- God instantly forgave all your past sins (1 John 1:9).
- He adopted you into His spiritual family (Ephesians 1:4–5).
- He gave you eternal life (John 3:16).
- He sent the Holy Spirit to give you assurance of your salvation (Romans 8:16).

When you became a Christian, you began a new life. What a wonderful experience!

But remember, you are on a journey. You can't camp out here. There are many steps ahead, and you'll want to keep making progress toward your goal of becoming a completely new person.

The Bible puts it this way, "For you were once darkness, but now you are light in the Lord. Live [walk] as children of light (for the fruit of the light consists in all goodness, righteousness and truth) and find out what pleases the Lord" (Ephesians 5: 8-10).

What emotions did you experience when you accepted Christ?

What has changed in your life since you took that first step?

What things in your life have not yet changed?

What *Didn't* Happen When *You* Became A *Christian*

Soon after you started your journey with Christ, you probably discovered that life still has a lot of challenges. You didn't become perfect overnight. There are still hills to climb, valleys to cross, and storms to endure. By now you've learned that becoming a Christian didn't remove all the problems from your life.

Of course, the biggest problem of all is within you: it is your own inherent sinfulness. When you became a Christian, God forgave your sins, but the desire to sin remained in your heart. You still face the temptation to return to your old way of life. In your heart, you can feel something that wants to respond to those temptations. Some of the old weaknesses that you used to feel are still hanging around. Perhaps they seem even more bothersome than before.

There may even be times when you wonder if you can keep going on this new road. You may feel inadequate to live the kind of

life God expects. Temptation seems so overwhelming at times that you feel helpless to resist. "What's the use?" you may have wondered. "No matter how hard I try, I seem to fail."

Although you are grateful that God has forgiven your sins, you probably realize that you are not yet free from sin's power. Undoubtedly, you have longed for God to do something more so you can live more consistently and be more effective in your spiritual life.

What is your greatest weakness?

Which temptation seems to bother you the most?

Have you ever felt helpless or inadequate to live the good life that God seems to expect?

What *God Wants* For *You*

God doesn't want you to fail in your new life. He wants you to be fully transformed into a new and different person. You are God's child. As such, here are some of the things He wants for you. He wants you—

- To become mature and strong in your faith.
- To be able to overcome the temptations that sneak up on you.
- To grow deeper in your love for Him and for others.
- To live a life characterized by love, joy, peace, patience, kindness, goodness, faithfulness, gentleness, and self-control.

God wants you to become *Christlike;* that is, like His Son, Jesus Christ. According to the Bible, that is God's expectation for every Christian: "This is how we know we are in Him: whoever claims to live in Him must walk as Jesus did" (1 John 2:5–6). As if that weren't clear enough, God also gave this command: "Be holy, because I am holy" (1 Peter 1:16). God wants us to have the same motivations, attitudes, and behaviors as His Son, Jesus.

That's exciting, but it can also be intimidating. It looks as if God wants something from us that we simply cannot produce.

That's exactly right. You cannot change your inner nature; only God can do that. In order to take your next step, you must realize that you need God's help.

You see, when you accepted Christ, you received the benefit of what God had already done *for* you. Now God wants to do something *in* you—change your heart. Are you ready?

As you read God's Word, what expectations do you see that God has for you?

Would other people say there are ways in which your life reflects Jesus Christ? What are they?

In what ways is your life not a reflection of Jesus?

The *Holy Spirit* Helps You *Grow*

What God expects from you, He will enable you to do. He has promised that He will free you from the penalty and the power of sin so that you can fully be the person He wants you to be.

God freed you from the penalty of sin when He forgave you. But the power of sin is still at work in your life. There is something inside you that is responsive to temptation and may even lead you back into sin. That's why you may often feel powerless about your behavior. You know what is right, and you want to do it, but you can't. That cycle of failure results from your inner nature, which is basically sinful (Ephesians 2:1–3).

God wants to change that. He promises to cleanse your sinful nature and to plant His divine nature within you. The Bible says, "His divine power has given us everything we need for life and godliness. . . . He has given us His very great and precious promises, so that through them you may participate in the divine nature and escape the corruption in the world caused by evil desires" (2 Peter 1:3–4).

Imagine! You can be changed from within so that your heart will willingly obey God's will.

FREEDOM

Does it sometimes feel that there is a war between good and evil taking place in your heart?

What would your life be like if you were freed from the power of sin?

How This Happens

As a believer in Christ, you are no longer guilty for your past sins. *Justification* was when God, based on Christ's death on the cross, freed you from the penalty of sin.

Sanctification is when God frees you from the power of sin by cleansing your heart and setting you apart for a special, holy purpose. God sanctifies us through the power of the Holy Spirit.

You can see both of those actions mentioned in a single verse of Scripture, 1 John 1:9: "If we confess our sins, He is faithful and just and will forgive us our sins [justification] and purify us from all unrighteousness [sanctification]."

Just before Jesus left the earth, He told His disciples that they would soon receive a special gift. He said, "In a few days you will be baptized with the Holy Spirit. . . . you will receive power when the Holy Spirit comes on you; and you will be my witnesses" (Acts 1:5, 8).

God has promised the same gift to you. You received the Holy Spirit at the moment you put your trust in Christ. That's when the Spirit began His cleansing and empowering work in you. When the Spirit's work is complete, your sinful nature will be cleansed and you will be empowered to live an effective Christian life.

What evidence of the Holy Spirit's work have you seen in your life?

Would you say that the Holy Spirit now occupies every area of your life, or only a part?

Do you ever have a hunger for more of God?

HOLY SPIRIT

What *You Can* Do To *Cooperate* With God

God always accomplishes His work in us through our response of faith. Faith is accepting the promise of God and committing ourselves to partner with Him.

So the first thing God wants you to do is commit yourself completely to Him. When you insist on maintaining ownership of your life, you can quickly lose control. That's because your sin nature is really in command. In order to live a Christlike life, you must first surrender your will and the control of your life to Him.

This is really a death experience. You must be willing to leave behind old habits and old ways of living, and surrender every area of your life to God. The Bible says, "Put to death, therefore, whatever belongs to your earthly nature: sexual immorality, impurity, lust, evil desires and greed, which is idolatry. . . .You used to walk in these ways, in the life you once lived" (Colossians 3:5, 7).

PARTN

God wants to occupy every area of your heart through His Holy Spirit. Only then can He fully cleanse your sinful nature. For that to happen, you must choose to set your affections on God alone.

Is there some area of your life that you have kept private, hidden even from God?

Are you prepared to surrender your whole life to God?

TIMING

When You Can *Expect* This To *Happen*

Becoming a Spirit-filled, sanctified person began the day you accepted Christ as your savior. God has been at work in your heart since that moment, and His goal is nothing less than your complete transformation. The Bible says, "He [God] who began a good work in you will carry it on to completion until the day of Christ Jesus" (Philippians. 1:6).

Whenever you realize your need and are willing to surrender yourself completely to Him, God is willing to take the next step in cleansing and empowering you. It may take awhile, however, for you to see all the areas of your life that are not pleasing to God and that need His cleansing. The Holy Spirit will help you with that. It's the Spirit's job to turn on the lights in the closets of your life, exposing areas that need to be opened up and cleaned out. That started when you took your first step of faith. It will be more complete when you take the step of surrendering your life fully to God and accepting the cleansing of the Holy Spirit.

Living a holy (sanctified) life sounds like it is intended for people in monasteries or for older folk in rocking chairs. But living like Christ should characterize your journey right now—regardless of where you live and work or how old you are.

Yes, you will make some missteps along the way. But because of the Holy Spirit's work, your heart may be perfectly set on Christ and your motives may always be pure. Ultimate perfection will come only when you enter heaven. That will be your final step. Meanwhile, your next step awaits. God is ready to fill every area of your life with His Spirit, cleanse your sinful nature, and empower you to live a full and effective life.

Are you ready to take the step?

Taking the Next Step

God is leading you into His next big step for you—the sanctified, Spirit-filled life. You need to cooperate with Him by—

- Allowing Him to be on the throne of your life.
- Letting go of everything that represents sin in your life.
- Choosing to love God with all of your heart.

He will then be able to—

- Fill you completely with His Holy Spirit.
- Fully cleanse your heart from sin.
- Enable you to love Him and others with a pure love.
- Strengthen you to resist temptation.

RESPONSE

Remember, God always works in partnership with your faith. You hold the key that opens the door to each room of your life. When you surrender that control to God, allowing Him complete access to your heart, the Holy Spirit will finally be free to cleanse and empower you fully. You will be able to live a Christlike life.

Yes, Heavenly Father, I want to have a pure heart. I am ready to take the next step by surrendering every area of my life to You. On this day I totally commit my life to Christ and open every hidden area of my heart to the Holy Spirit. I pray that You will change my heart, cleansing me of any thought, motive, or action that is contrary to Your will. Give me the power to walk as Jesus walked and to live a life that is pleasing to You in every way. Amen.

______________________________ ______________

Signature *Date*

What the Bible Says About the Your Next Step

The Need for Holiness

But just as he who called you is holy, so be holy in all you do; for it is written: "Be holy, because I am holy." —1 Peter 1:15–16

Make every effort to live in peace with all men and to be holy; without holiness no one will see the Lord.

—Hebrews 12:14

God's Promise of Cleansing

It is God's will that you should be sanctified. . . .

—1 Thessalonians 4:3

May God himself, the God of peace, sanctify you through and through. May your whole spirit, soul and body be kept blameless at the coming of our Lord Jesus Christ.

—1 Thessalonians 5:23

Surrendering to God

Just as you used to offer the parts of your body in slavery to impurity and to ever-increasing wickedness, so now offer them in slavery to righteousness leading to holiness.

—Romans 6:19